HALF
PRICE
Poo
08 -
067

pocket
universe

poems

pocket universe

Nancy Reddy

Louisiana State University Press   *Baton Rouge*

Published by Louisiana State University Press
lsupress.org

Copyright © 2022 by Nancy Reddy
All rights reserved. Except in the case of brief quotations used in articles
or reviews, no part of this publication may be reproduced or transmitted in
any format or by any means without written permission of Louisiana State
University Press.

LSU Press Paperback Original

DESIGNER: Michelle A. Neustrom
TYPEFACE: Arno Pro

COVER IMAGE: *Where I Send My Awareness,* 2019, by Kate Walters

LIBRARY OF CONGRESS CATALOGING-IN-PUBLICATION DATA
Names: Reddy, Nancy, 1982– author.
Title: Pocket universe : poems / Nancy Reddy.
Description: Baton Rouge : Louisiana State University Press, [2022]
Identifiers: LCCN 2021019081 (print) | LCCN 2021019082 (ebook) |
    ISBN 978-0-8071-7583-5 (paperback) | ISBN 978-0-8071-7702-0 (pdf) |
    ISBN 978-0-8071-7703-7 (epub)
Classification: LCC PS3618.E4269 P63 2022 (print) | LCC PS3618.E4269
    (ebook) | DDC 811/.6—dc23
LC record available at https://lccn.loc.gov/2021019081
LC ebook record available at https://lccn.loc.gov/2021019082

contents

III

IV

I

In the Hôtel-Dieu

Paris, sixteenth century

In the *salle sauvage,* in the animal body of labor, women labored, slept, recovered,
    up to five in a bed. Book-trained doctors delivered women of their babies

with hands still slick and stained from the autopsied bodies of mothers who'd died
    hours earlier of childbed fever inside the same hot rooms. The doctors

blamed the mothers for their fevers: their split-open bodies were filled with pus,
    and the men saw milk gone wandering, rotten, clotted

in the abdomen and intestines. The doctors blamed the women's shame,
    their worry, the lack of fresh air, the sewer gas. They filled the wards

with smoke to purify the air, baked linens, and walked unwashed
    between delivery room and morgue.

There are rooms where a woman's rickets-narrowed pelvis is displayed in brine,
    where baby girls joined at the hip swim in a jar,

where a fetal skeleton is passed through a pelvic basin to show how birth
    is meant to work. The doctors were taught to deliver without looking,

shielded by sheets draped over mother and physician.
    The women labor flat-backed in the stirruped position

named for stones. The doctors wield forceps, from the Latin for
    hot and *seize,* the paired spoons that scoop the baby from the birth canal.

Yanked from where I'd lodged inside my mother's narrow hips,
    collarbone broken, but alive, redheaded, howling,
        I was born like that.

The Thing (1982)

In the year I'm trying to be born,
Kurt Russell takes a flamethrower to his friends
because they'd become monsters in the shape of men.
Something buried in the tundra 100,000 years heats up
and so the movie starts in ice and ends in burning,
two survivors drinking around a fire
while camp burns down behind them. When the year opens,
Margaret Thatcher's son disappears in the Sahara
and reappears three days later. The first computer virus
travels via floppy disk. In Utah, a retired dentist
receives the first permanent artificial heart
and lives into the new year. It's the year my father leaves
to hike a New Hampshire mountain and ski down
the ungroomed ravine. There's a war
and then another war. In photos from the time
my mother's hair is short and dark. In another photo
I sleep against my father's chest
as he sleeps on the couch. The thing is,
there are no pictures of the three of us together,
which is how I know my father carries even then
his leaving. When the camera leaves them
we can't say for sure which man's the monster in the snow,
but we know that they won't live for long. Russell's face is framed
by a fur-lined coat, tendrils of snot frozen in his mustache,
and when he says *I know I'm me,* we can choose
if we believe him or we don't. We lived then in the small brick ranch
perched on a hill above the steakhouse with a life-sized plaster Holstein
standing on its roof. Even in those earliest months I slept alone,
belly down on a crib stacked with handstitched quilts,
headlights of passing cars streaking across the bedtime walls.

Feast Day

The world has always been
this bloody. St. Justus was nine
when he was reported
as a Christian. Beheaded, he held
his head in his hands. My grandmother
confessed, as doctrine willed it, weekly.
She was so good, and always right.
What could she have confessed? She knew
the name for every kind of fork
and where to place each one
for the dinner party. The Devil for her
was real perhaps but impolite
to speak of, God a disapproving uncle
you'd do your best not to disappoint.
Which saint could she have prayed to
when her first daughter, days old,
died for no reason? When, years later,
she woke from another birth with no womb
to bear more children? Impolite
to speak of the body and its openings
and its failures. At seventy and seventy-five
she spoke still of driving an elderly friend
to the doctor, but by eighty she'd grown tired
of opening the paper each morning
to find her friends in the obituaries. Each saint
is feasted on their *dies natalis,* the birth
into the next life. It was my birthday
the day my grandmother died, and so now
we share the day with St. Liberata, St. Gwen,
and St. Luke, whose gospel is the only one
to tell the story of the Annunciation. The saints
can't touch us, or else they're ineffectual,

or unjust. Confession doesn't count
if you say it only to yourself. The first daughter's name
is my name. My grandmother wrote
her own obituary, and when the paper ran it
not one of us knew what that missing baby's middle initial
stood for. There was no one left to ask.

First Light

Astronomers tilt the telescope to gaze at distant galaxies,
and we can see the early universe in the light that finally finds us:

the blue-streaked whorls of hydrogen, the knotted
newborn stars. The universe was, for millions of years,

full only of the darkest dark, the just-born elements clustering
and joining, until all at once, like the bright quick heat

of a good idea or a dividing cell: starlight,
and all the heavy atoms that give us this good life

formed inside those blazing short-lived stars. We can only see
the places in the universe the light has touched. We have to learn

to look, the way that, one October afternoon, I lay against
the crinkling paper of the exam table while the nurse

swabbed gel across my belly, and in the night sky
of the uterus, on the grayscale screen of a handheld sonogram,

we saw it all at once: the striations of muscle and space,
the stuttering and blinking, the insistent flicker of a beating heart.

New Year New You

For a long time,
there was nothing, then
there wasn't
nothing. The universe
is mostly mechanical,
Cartesian clockwork
ticking while
the gears itch
in a locked box. Kepler
believed in a god
who made the world
and left us here. Through
Christmas Eve
and Christmas Day
I lay in bed, bleeding
and watching *Mad Men*,
staying still
to keep the baby safe.
Lucretius believed
we are all made
of primordial
goop. *We know nothing*
about a body
until we know
what it can do.
I bled and bled and
the baby didn't die
and the new year
split us open.

Tin Anniversary

We were married
by a judge inside a chapel
at a stained-glass altar
with no Christ watching over us, no
sacramental blessing. The only time
we'd both stepped foot inside a church,
I was a bridesmaid in David's Bridal satin,
my hair Aqua Netted and pinned at JC Penney's,
and you sat in the back pew, handsome
in your one dark suit. All the assembled watched
the happy couple walk with hands bound
to kneel and pray before the Virgin Mary
as in an ancient tragedy where all the best magic
takes place offstage. We were so young then,
years away still from our own vows.
When my mother's mother married
she changed her name and cut her hair. She moved
across state lines and called home on Sundays
to ask her childhood cook
how to roast a chicken. She was that
kind of a wife. I was the second wife.
My father walked me down the aisle to the altar
and when it came time
to face the officiant,
I gave myself.

The Sun King Invents Stirruped Birth

The queen's anointed body
can't be touched by common hands. She labors
in a draped room where women tend her,
the doctor sheeted and concealed. We forget now

how small they were, how poor
before the riches of the new world
turned the old world golden. The king wants
the world revealed. His mistress

is cloaked in fine cloth but proximate, her body
a display case. He has his doctors
hold her open so that he can see inside her
when the baby's coming. The speculum

is born this way. She labors, watched and spread.
She labors on her back for better looking. There are no limits
to how and when and where a king can look.

∽

In the history written by a man, the mistress (there were many)
goes unnamed. It was most likely Louise de la Vallière, who bore
five children to the king, of whom only the last two lived past
infancy. The pregnancies are staggeringly close. She gave birth
sometimes twice in the same year. To conceive again that quickly
her babies must have been taken to the wet nurse immediately
after birth.

∽

Louis XIV waged war
after war and when he finally died
his debt-crippled, famine-hunted subjects
jeered the funeral procession as it passed.

Painless Childbirth

Remedies include chloroform and whiskey;
also distraction, belly rubs, cloths soaked in warm oil.
Pliny the Elder suggested a tonic of ground snails,
earthworms, dissolved droppings of geese. Some made belly salves
of viper fat, eel gall, powdered donkey hoof, the tongues of snakes,
chameleons, rabbits. Henbane, hemlock, mandrake
all bring mild pain relief but also sometimes
seizures, paralysis, coma, death.

Twilight

labored in darkness   not without pain but with   no memory of pain
    woke up a mother   woke up when the nurses
brought the scrubbed   and bundled baby to her and for days

        she swore it wasn't hers   primates lick the amniotic fluid
from the dirt where the birthing mother spills it   fight for the rich meat
    of the placenta   mammals know their babies   by their scent

this birth smells only of   scopolamine   linoleum   ammonia

The Russian Method

When we think of Pavlov's dogs
we forget the women he trained

to pant through their labors,
to birth their babies without pain. In the last weeks

I sat heavy in the chair I planned to use for nursing
and dozed as the CDs promising self-hypnosis

droned through headphones. Sometimes I fell
into a cooling blankness that was nothing like

the work of labor. Asked about the Russian Method
for painless birth, Pope Pius XII answered, "there are some who allege

that originally childbirth was entirely painless
and that it became painful only at a later date,"

as if the pain of birth was occasioned only
by an error in God's word

or how we heard it. Queen Victoria, who had nine children,
loved her husband and hated pregnancies and babies.

She delivered seven before the miracle of twilight sleep
and two more after. She said, "I think much more

of being like a cow or a dog at such moments, when our poor nature
becomes so very animal and unecstatic." In late labor,

each contraction pulses the baby's blood from the placenta
to the branching blood vessels in the lungs,

flushing amniotic fluid for the baby's first breath.

Everything Is Animals

everything is pitch-black   then everything is high-gloss
    the hot dense descent   the wrenching waves and then their wake:
    the pain and then   the shadow of

an unscalable crest   but the body   scales it anyway

word-stripped inside the pain   she thinks *there has to be a better way*   she thinks
    help I can't—help—

and then her body   a split star   then the baby:

    hello stranger, mother thinks. *hello, you.*

Golden Hour

When they lift the baby to my chest, his skin's still slick
with clots of vernix. The soft plates of his skull
are compressed into a cone, and his dark hair is damp
with amniotic fluid. I inhale the unwashed funk
and watch my naked mammal root
and nuzzle, watch thick yellow colostrum
dribble from each nipple. For two days in recovery
we're tended, measured, fed, and fussed over. The baby
barely cries from his tiny toothless mouth. Fireworks
crackle somewhere in the distance. He wakes once
in the night and I hold his swaddled body
in the gray light. In the hospital I'm a good mother.

II

Postpartum

It doesn't feel holy. The days are jagged and raw, my body
a puffed sack, the nights a stripped-off skin. The baby teaches me

I am not what I thought. Not patient, not loving, not
an endless fount of joy. I'm a spigot. I'm a body

holding a body but we're strangers to each other. I don't feel
like anyone's mother. He lifts his head, then drops it down against

my collarbone, then screams. I'd thought that motherhood would be
a good machine, a wheel and pulley whooshing out the dark

and sinful parts of me, leaving only love for baby's doughy hands,
his lightbulb toes. I'm the bad one. I'm a sack of rot. I'd thought

that when the baby came I'd be myself but better.

Your Best Post-Baby Body

Two days after giving birth, my empty belly flopped so tenderly
    in the bathroom mirror in the recovery suite. I was afraid

to shit or take a shower because I wasn't sure
                what had happened to me or if the stitches
would rip. I'd heard women say *down there* would look like meat

so for weeks I didn't look. When Christ came back

        he got to keep his scars. He flashed his stigmata
at the women at the tomb
            and they knew him as their risen Lord. Three days

inside the earth. Two months after giving birth
Heidi Klum walked a catwalk in angel wings. The tabloids tell you

        how she got her body back:
Tori Spelling joined Jenny Craig and lost the weight. J. Lo did her first triathlon
7 months after giving birth to twins. Gisele says, "Some women think

they can get pregnant and turn their body
        into a garbage disposal." Gisele walked the runway
in wings and a G-string six weeks after an ecstatic

natural birth. Natural is one way not to say
vagina in mixed company. The girl-saint loved the Lord

and then she wouldn't eat
        is every story.
Christina loved the Lord
        and turned splinter-thin. She loved him
right up out of her body, her stigmata visible

only to herself. And through that long cold-bodied death, Christ never
learned to listen. "This body is the site of a miracle,"
says Kerry Washington. Kerry Washington does 6 a.m. pilates

while her daughter sleeps. In the recovery room
I'm a stretched and sagging balloon. When I get my body back
all the parts are rearranged and worn. When I get my
body back it's not quite mine.

Anatomical Venus

The girl sliced open. The pearl necklace at her throat, organs unfurled like upholstery. I don't want to be meat. I don't want to be a star lit by rage. Six weeks postpartum, cleared for exercise and sex, I run the leafy sidewalks of my neighborhood, boobs flapping in a gray pre-pregnancy bra. I run away from my baby, away from my indoor life, and before I've gotten to the park, I've peed my blue pants navy. I don't want to be a mother if it means I can't keep my body inside my body. Inside every Anatomical Venus, a perfect fetus, like the secret that was the whole point all along.

The Nature of Love

When a man wants to learn about love
he builds a pair of monkey mothers
and places them in wire cages.

One mother's made of metal, one of cloth.
The babies love the cloth mother and cling to her,
even when they nurse from metal. At first

the mothers have no faces, just milky orbs,
and the babies love them better like that. Days old,
a baby curls against the cloth mother's warm base.

Each mother's perfect in her loneliness, mute
inside the watched cage. The scientists
give the mothers painted eyes and mouths

and the babies turn them blank again. The babies
spin the faces back around, reach up to palm
the changeless face that first stared down at them.

The laboratory's lined with cages. The babies
touch the mothers who cannot touch them back.
Lab assistants chart the times. A visiting reporter asks, *What is*

the nature of love? Love's an easy word. Liars use it.
So do thieves. What Harlow's found is labor,
the dumb and ceaseless work of mothering

a thing too small and new to love you back.
I'd thought I'd be a better mother.
When again my sleep is split by cries

it's despair I feel, not love. I take my body
to the baby in the dark.
When I lift him from the crib he doesn't know me

until I brush a nipple across his cheeks and lips.
He roots and latches. It's not quite love.
I'm cloth and I drip milk.

We're animals together in the night.
The crib's slats cast a shadow across both our bodies.

The Braided Stream

It's easy to forget, when the news shows two smiling children,
that you're looking at the dead. An actress is found buried

in the backyard of her London home, her sons
in shallow graves beside her. They spent three weeks
in the earth before forensics came in and raised them up again.

A continent away, their killer drinks beer in the sun.
On that same continent, cradle of humanity, a cave
deep in the earth is found filled with skeletons, proof
our ancestors learned to bury their dead. They had no words,

no way of saying *mother, lover, son,* but they carried
their loved bodies through a dark lit by torches. They knew
the living and the dead could not stay long together.
They knew they could not leave their dead

beneath the open sky. The bodies
found deep inside the earth aren't human, not yet.
They have shoulders and hands built for climbing,
lower limbs for walking. They touch the earth

and it transforms them. And here, inside the earth:
mandible, ribs, bones of inner ear, the vertebrae
of infants thin as thimbles.

And here the fossil record falls apart. In London
children's bodies turn to earth. In tabloids they wear jackets,
the fleece hoods framing smiling faces. Their mother

had left television to become a teacher. She couldn't
keep her children safe. The coroner says he broke their necks. And then
he buried them. For tenderness, to give their bodies
a safe and quiet home? or just

to smooth his flight? When he's found hiding
he tries to ward off capture with a knife and spoon. He won't smile
for the cameras but he won't say he's sorry either. Before we were human

we knew to carry the dead away from the living
and place their bodies deep inside a cave named for stars.

Goodnight Mother, Goodnight Moon

We're in a place where words don't work.

The painters tarp the windows
                          and the air inside the house goes gauzy.

The crying baby shakes the house. The baby's face red and wild
he's sweating in the swaddle. His eyes are sealed. The baby has no mother

yet. The air inside the house rubbed raw.

The painters circle the house in hazmat suits,
        chipping flakes of blue lead paint into the yard. We're haloed by harm.

℈

When the baby finally sleeps the house seals itself like an envelope.

The mother scours the kitchen for something sweet,
cracking a sugar-crusted muffin against her teeth. Asleep

the baby is a solid mass of muslin, spittle, milk. Where does the baby go
in sleep? Does he dream himself

        a better mother? Does another woman hold him
down the long cool hallway of his dream life?

℈

A mother is a body. The mother is a body for the baby. She leaks

and spurts. Her parts are unreliable and worn. The mother's body
        has no private places.

In bed the mother tries to remember how it felt when the baby swam inside her.

She lays on her back and feels the soft space in her belly,
the two-finger gap in abdominal wall where her body split

so he could grow. He has his own skin now, lungs that billow and contract
like paired fluttering miracles.

The mother loves the baby
and also she can't finish a sentence. Her mind reaches the frayed end of a thought

and the verb falls out of reach.

 Friends when they visit seem to travel in
from a foreign country of sleep.

ↄ⌐

The baby cries when the mother leaves the room. Which must mean that she exists,
 if she can be missed.

ↄ⌐

Now she's sobbing in the produce section, picking through a box of bell peppers,
 their skins gone loose and soft. Now it's morning,

 the daytime baby cooing in his bassinet. She touches her nose
to his pursed damp lips and inhales.

ↄ⌐

The mother wakes in the night. The dark is a belly. She tosses inside it.
Headlights flash through the window. Dark again then.
The baked bread smell of sleeping baby in the mother's room. When she wakes

the sheets are soaked, the sugar of spilled milk
crystallized against the pillowcase. The room is dark. The baby's breathing

somewhere out of reach.

Ghosts in the Nursery

Black walnuts turn the soil to acid
so nothing else can grow. I'm inside
learning letdown, though it doesn't feel
like the sharp tug or burn or rush
of milk the mommies on the internet describe.
I know it's working only when I see
the baby's throat moving to swallow
beneath his rattlesnake jaw, the latch
that hooks my whole nipple between his gums.
Squirrels split black walnut shells by throwing them
from tree branches onto the cracked concrete walkway,
then clawing out the meat with their dainty
almost-human hands. Their furred tails
like fishing lures. Ghosts flood the nursery:
bad spirits, guardian angels, better older sisters, all the
Instamommies who are photogenic
even in calamity. The last ghost to leave
is the mother's own.

Fable

Sambisa Forest, Nigeria

The forest here is made of girls
and automatic weapons. A sparrow calls
across a thicket of brushwood. The antelope gather

but not like warnings. When peacekeepers
come searching for the stolen girls,
the men hide the girls beneath the earth. Should this look

more like violence? The flatland is knotted
with groves of acacia, mesquite, wild black plum,
clots of thornbushes too dense for flight. The story

༂

splinters out. Two girls leapt from the lorry
before it reached the forest. They sleep beneath stars
in the forked base of a red bushwillow. A velvet silence

wraps them. At home their brothers split seasoned logs
of trees like this, peeled the pale sapwood
to reveal the core of sky-gray

heartwood good for charcoal and fires. The girls wake
and find a shepherd to carry the hurt girl home
across the handlebars of his bicycle. Inside the forest

༂

the girls are told to choose: be made a bride,
or be a slave. A husband wraps his wife
in cloth and soon they have a son. When she's rescued

the women at home hate her. They call her war bride,
and worse. No one touches her son's feet.
She stays covered and at night, in the heat,

a snake comes into the compound
and the boy is killed before he's even reached a year.
The collared dove has a pale belly, pinkish white.

The feathers it uses in flight are nearly black.
It's the wild ancestor of the domestic dove
who's held in cages elsewhere. The girls

are girls, their bodies porous
and woundable. The animals
can't help them.

Ordinary Pleasure

The nursing baby thumps my breast above the nipple
       with his fist, as if to make the milk come faster.
           He curls his hand into my hair and yanks,

then finally slows and sleeps, his eyelids closing
       like a precious doll I had in childhood, his eyelashes
           so long and blond, against his sleeping cheeks

and it is the perfect moment of my life,
       the baby who sleeps against my belly, where he first
           fed and grew and kicked,

like the dream of a better, sweeter self.
       In Michigan, a mother fills her toddler with Benadryl
           and when she's sleeping soundly

holds a pillow to her face and presses down
       until the girl stops breathing. Then the mother swallows pills
           and lays down in a graveyard to die

but wakes instead, stricken and childless. In Oregon,
       a mother tosses her six-year-old son from a bridge
           and his bones splinter when they hit the river.

In Los Angeles, two days after Thanksgiving, two girls find a day-old baby
       buried under chipped asphalt, wailing.
           He's wrapped in a hospital blanket

and the mother who left him must still have been bleeding,
       leaking milk. Women's violence is like this,
           intimate and bodily. Poisonings,

not gunshots. The baby is so small. His lips
        are pursed in sleep, his puffed cheeks still pink. He is small
          and I am huge. I hold his whole life

in my arms, and I am so unbearably, terribly strong.

The Good Enough Mother

The baby cries   because its mother
doesn't know   how to hold it right. Holding

is a form of love. The good enough
        mother is reliable.   She merges with the infant.
There are those   who can hold an infant

and those who cannot. A good   enough mother

can be taught to do better.   Who holds
        the mother. If   the mother isn't   good
enough   the baby cries. Some mothers

can't be helped.

A Good Comfortable Road

> But as I have always held it a crime to anticipate evils I will believe it is a
> good comfortable road until I am compelled to believe differently.
>
> —MERIWETHER LEWIS, upon seeing the Rocky Mountains
> for the first time, May 26, 1805

The day requires a shape.
    We dress. I pour coffee in a travel mug,
snap the infant car seat in the stroller base, then bundle baby in
    and snap the five-point harness into place. It's snug,

just like the nurses at the hospital showed me,
    no more than two fingers between the strap and baby's skin. We stroll.
    The baby wails beneath the stroller's visor,
or else he sleeps. The sidewalk ridges up where tree roots rumble through,
    the stroller jolts and jostles baby.

The neighbors' tulips finally spiking up through mulch
    but not yet blooming, another neighbor's prayer flags
flapping in the breeze. The retirees sit on folding chairs
    inside their cool garage and wave. Lewis had faith in a good road,

friendly natives, flora and fauna in abundance. They found a new coast
    and for once didn't name it for themselves.
The guide's wife went into labor in year one. To ease her pain
    they made a potion from a rattlesnake's rattle

and she birthed a boy. She carried him the whole way to the coast.
    A statue shows it, the cloth-wrapped baby on her back, surveying.
    Lewis made it back to Missouri after all,
accumulated ruinous debt, shot himself in a boarding house,
    and bled out on a buffalo hide robe. The new world's not

an unmixed blessing. Light through the new leaves
        make shapes across the baby's hands. He waves them

and we learn each other like this, walking.
        Later, when I look at pictures of this time, I'll see the baby as a mouth.
For weeks every time I lifted him
            he wailed to nurse. I couldn't hold him

without opening my body to him like a faucet. None of the photos
        show me all day in a dark room

holding a crying baby while I cry and pat his back with useless palms.
        Not one will show me, when the baby finally sleeps, standing in the doorway
watching his breathing as I weep. For now
            the air is light and cool, the grass along the sidewalk
            tipped with dew.

My Sentimental Baby

When I say the new baby's breath is *milk sweet,*
please know I'm speaking also of my swollen
lumpen tits, the spit and lanolin, the leaking
milk that's dried around the aureola, the ducts
the milk shot through to where it meets
the baby's flanged lips. Know that breastmilk
is made of blood. Inside my breasts the alveoli
branch from milk ducts like buds too tightly furled
to blossom, but with a good deep latch
my nipple's stretched until it's pressed
against the soft palate in the back of the baby's mouth.
His toothless gums compress the whole breast and
he swallows. When I can't stop huffing
the baby's head, the spongy scalp and fontanel,
the flaking cradle cap, I'm smelling
the inside of my own body, the uterus and caul
and amniotic fluid, the birth canal he traveled.
When I'm falling in mammal love with this new creature,
maybe I'll catch some of that love, too. If the words I use
to tell you how I love the silken loose-boned heft
of this baby sleeping on my chest
feel "processed" or 'less than fresh," I'll tell you this: I built
this baby in my body from nearly nothing
and nursed him with the milk my body made.
I'll use the words and tools I have at hand.

III

Naming the World

When he's past a year, then 18 months and still not speaking, we begin
      to teach the baby signs,
             scooping the air in front of us for *want,*
      circling a fist over our hearts for *please.* It's *more* he uses most,
gathering the fingers on each hand together, then touching the fingertips
over and over and over. At meals we ask
      more cheese, or more turkey?
                more banana or more cracker?
holding each item in the air so he can learn to choose,
      trying to tie the sounds of words to the objects that he wants.
The signs go general and in excitement he signs
more and more, more water in the bath, more blocks, more
      milk, more dancing. Without a word to stitch it to, the sign's sometimes
hard to parse. Sometimes it seems it's just a baby way of saying
      joy. More dogs, more snow, more plastic t-rex stomping
over train tracks. Sitting on the floor with the new baby kicking at my ribs,
this wondrous not-quite baby smiling at his trains,
      baby, *yes,* more of this. More of all of it.

The End of Limbo

In the *Divine Comedy,* purgatory was a pastoral, a grove
of meadows, streams, and castles. Those who repented late

had the farthest to climb but could still hope. I am sitting
in this hotel room below a sign that promises to guide me to the exit,

that promises Your Safety in an Emergency. The sign says
In Case of Fire, Do Not Panic. Do Not Use the Elevators. In medieval art

the damned raise their arms through flames to call for blessings
from the Virgin Mary and her infant son, just one drop of water

to cool the burning. Long before my birth, the worst thing happened:
the first baby my grandmother gave birth to died, days old, for no reason.

The baby had been named but not yet baptized, so where could her soul go
when her newborn body went in the ground? But that mother

didn't die, didn't turn her back on God. She went on each morning
making eggs and bacon for a husband who rarely spoke

between the bites of buttered toast, she scrubbed the floors
and learned to make a roast. She gave birth to three more daughters

and the last of them gave birth to me and named me for the daughter
who'd been lost first. And all that time, where was that still- and always-baby?

The church of my childhood taught that all the unbaptized
went to limbo, where they could repent, make penance,

and wait patiently until they, too, could be forgiven. The church
of my childhood taught that every sin could be washed clean,

except the sin of loss of faith. When the Lord stopped speaking to me
I didn't miss Him for a long time. I was busy, grading papers and falling in love

and going to yoga. When I sit at my sister's table and hold hands for the blessing
I am not moved. There is still, I suppose, the specific theological question

of heaven and who gets in and where to find it. Following the logic
of a law-abiding God, St. Augustine saw those babies sent to hell

but granted one slight mercy: they suffered only *the mildest condemnation*.
St. Thomas Aquinas believed unbaptized babies would never

see heaven but also that they wouldn't know to miss it. When the errorless Church
changed the law on purgatory it was presented as not mistake but revelation.

The commission offered *serious liturgical and theological grounds for hope* that
all the blameless held in purgatory through no fault of their own might be

whooshed through after all. My grandmother never spoke her first daughter's name
except when calling me. The ghosts of all those women

gather above me as I kiss my own babies sleeping safe inside their beds.

And Not By Sight

I wake in the dark,
the new baby kicking in my belly, my son asleep
across the hall. No one's dead. Still,
I see the bodies everywhere:

one boy shot down in a playground, another
        facedown on a beach. I can't look
and can't stop looking. Why should I be spared?

      Half-waking in the dark, I see
baby belly puffed out in the bath, laughing,
      the small pink spots along his insteps
         where new shoes rubbed skin raw, see his sweet face
slipping under. I blink hard to clear the vision. If he were dead

he wouldn't be in that body. I don't believe in God,
so he wouldn't be waiting for me elsewhere, either. He'd just
      be dead, but I know that if I had to send

his perfect body into the earth, I'd bundle my own body
      in beside him. At the viewing. my mother
laid a cream cashmere wrap
across her mother in the casket. *I didn't want her to be cold,*
      she said. Now, years later, no one's dead. I'm sitting

      in the driveway outside daycare, stuffed with tears,
thinking about shutting the baby in a box and sending him
into the ground alone. I don't believe he's only

in his body. But where is he, then? He can't speak yet
to say, and if he walked down the street alone, he'd just
    be gone, not yet able
to name himself home. I love him

        with my hands. The air outside the car is so cold
it stings my chapped knuckles. He's safe inside,
    in a room that smells of spaghetti and syrup, tossing cars
down a plastic track. I go inside
    and hold him to be sure.

The Middle Sin

At daycare pickup, the young and gorgeous rabbi's wife
        walks her hand-holding daughters down the sidewalk
to their car. Though I know her real hair's hidden
        under a remarkably good wig,
the three of them, all redheads, are a clearly matching set
and watching one sister pull the other's curls,

        I feel again the lurch
when the sonogram again said *son*
        and quickly cancelled out a girlhood: no
little girl bangs and barrettes, no thick cotton tights over freckled legs:

        no daughter.

        The dizzy whirling sick of love and want. I snap my older son
into his car seat, kiss the soft globe
        of his cheek. The baby flaps his chubby fist. What wicked
luck. What foolishness and greed. Like begging someone's god
to see you in this blessed and lucky life and strike you down.

Taxonomy of Dads

Dads in cargo shorts in 40 degrees. Business casual dad. Dad in college sweatshirt. Grumpy minivan dad. Sensitive babywearing dad. Secret tattoo dad. Dad who touches all the moms on their backs or elbows in a slightly too familiar fashion. Dad of girl in princess outfit. Newly feminist dad of daughters. Feminist dad who at a meeting says *great idea!* to the male colleague who repeats from beneath a beard what a female colleague just said. Cross-fit dad. Bearded dad in Dogfish Head hoodie. Dad who fucks his wife like he means it, and not just on Saturdays. Dads named John. Dads named Jeffrey not Jeff. Dads whose wives have been all touched out for years. Dad in loafers with jeans. Dad who doesn't mentally reallocate all the daycare dollars, all the hours spent in doctors' offices and soccer fields and back to school night to vacations in places with exotic names. Dad who does.

The Second First Year

Season of gulls dipping down over the bay of walking the double stroller home along the boardwalk
Season of no sleep   Season of onesies   of rolling over and sitting up

Season of pump parts and rubber nipples and nipples stretched like taffy in the baby's mouth

Season of the split latch of the nursing bra   and the split abdominal wall   where babies grew
Season of savage sleeplessness   Season of browned banana goo stuck on every surface   Season

of the baby grabs the dog's fur   the dog snaps the air   and everyone cries

Season of footie jammies, abandoned milk cups curdling   beside the radiators' thumping heat
Season of *goodnight, mama*   and a smack of a kiss for baby brother Season of screeching   Season

of *can't I just have one minute to myself*   Season of gummy grins

The baby's the big brother now and holds the baby's hand   inside his fist   The baby bounces
in the jumperoo   while big brother eats waffles   Season of two babies splashing in the tub

Season of   screaming on the drive to daycare   then crying on the way to work

Season of pulling up on the crib   the coffee table   the dog crate   kitchen island

Season of diapered baby   running headlong into waves   Season of toes in sand

Season of every surface a barely hidden danger   every moving part a harm   Season of *shhhh*

slipping through the hallways   when the babies finally fall asleep

The Universe Has a Temperature

In New Jersey, in the middle of last century,
   scientists pointed a telescope to the blank night sky

      and found something peering back: the combined heat
of the universe, left over from the Big Bang
    and spread evenly across space. It's 2.725 kelvin. In this century,

it's Monday morning in Atlantic City, and I'm driving my baby to the ER.
     He's been above 100 since he woke, his breathing
   slow and labored, dozing hot and heavy across my chest,

too sick to cry. We're driving down Pacific, ocean and boardwalk
   on our right, vacant storefronts and check-cashing shops
     and fried chicken joints along the left,

to the pediatric ER that shares a parking lot with Caesar's.
     Our bodies are proof

    of nothing special. We carry the five most common elements
inside us. Each of those elements were born inside the earliest
    stars, so hot and dense they made new life.

After Cocktail Hour

It's late July. The lawn is full
of photogenic children
running and yelling against a backdrop
of sunset, the promise
of ice cream and fireflies
like we're inside the kingdom
of a Hidden Valley Ranch ad. The wives
are wearing sundresses or sensible shorts,
the husbands are lined up beside them
in their flat-front khaki pants. One husband
brings back a glass of chardonnay,
a single bead of condensation
just beginning to drip down the stem
and, with the habit-formed intimacy
of two fingers to the inner arm,
the place where you'd find a pulse
or draw blood, hands it to his wife.
Someone's child is at the lawn's edge, crying
and the blond-bobbed wife, the child's mother,
sees her husband laughing nearby,
not looking. She steps into the high grass
to comfort the wailing child. Is every
marriage a little bit
a catalog of grievances?

Spooky Action at a Distance

In the Nashville airport, in gate C-84, in the industrial carpet
    and molded plastic seats where we all wait to be carried elsewhere,

            a baby sleeps against his mother's chest.

His right foot is froglegged up to meet his chest. He's that new, his body
    soft and curled as if to fit still the small space of the womb.

            The universe is thin. Even across this gate—

the cable news blaring disaster, the static of the PA system, the suitcases
    and duffle bags stacked between the seats—

I can feel that baby's weight against my body. If the universe is local

it's only touch that moves us.
        Einstein called it *spooky*,

the way that particles separated by vast distances could as if on cue
    snap their electrons into alignment.

    I've been reminded twice today already
of the terrible things that happen to children in cars. In Texas, in the pure

late-summer heat, in a Walmart parking lot, while all day shoppers glide in and out
    the automatic sliding doors, a baby is snapped safely inside his car seat,

    dying. This hurt travels across the ridges of the world. My sons

    are far from me, but I can still see their blue-green eyes,
their shins speckled with summer bruises. There's no water

elsewhere in our solar system, or else it's locked beneath a frozen ocean on a distant planet's moon.

The ache of these delicate bodies swims across space.

In this vast expanding universe of noise and silence
we wait to be called.

IV

A Universe Composed of Solely Light

Of all the things I didn't know before I did,
there's this: how, at bedtime, patting the babies
down to sleep feels like romance.

When the boy breathes *mama,*
or when the baby clamps his hands
against my cheeks and plants a damp-lipped open-
mouthed kiss, I'm here in a bodily love
with the babies my body made.

                      But what to say
of the husband? What name could praise enough
the man who rises in the middle of the night
without complaint—or, with occasional
cursing only—to comfort the crying baby

whose snot-crusted nostrils won't let him breathe?
The man I married could make a perfect daiquiri
and loved my ass in a corset and heels.
He had never changed a diaper.

                        And here we are,
love, inside the long future that we promised,
in the lavender light of 3 a.m., one baby
whimpering in his crib while the other's
a hot and restless heft between us in the bed.

On the First Night of the Afterlife

JKN, 1925–2010

After the funeral mass, after a meal of beef on wick and chardonnay
cushioned by the plush carpet at the Bradford Club,

your daughters said you were right then heading to a big date in heaven,
as if their daddy had been sitting all those years patiently in suit and tie,

waiting to rise and pull out your chair. The love I'd seen was mostly labor,
as on the days you'd go to volunteer at hospice but first made him a lunch plate

and cut the crusts off turkey on white, arranged the Lay's potato chips
in a crescent around the edge and sealed the whole thing with Saran Wrap.

Had he not learned, in heaven, how to spread mayonnaise
on his own white bread? Your daughters talked about the afterlife

like it was the lobby of the only passable restaurant left in town,
where the soup was always baked potato but at least the waitress

knew to make a vodka tonic, extra lime, before you even asked.
But in the real sky planets whirl unseen above us. They move

even when for days I forget to think of them, and even before
we'd named Jupiter's four Galilean moons, they orbited

an enormous and unfriendly planet. Who am I to say
what makes a marriage, what laws govern its ellipses?

The heavens aren't Heaven. I don't think we'll get to live
this lucky life again. I hope that on the first night of your next life

there's someone waiting to turn back your covers,
to wipe the cold cream gently from your cheek.

The Fifth Great Ape

By the time we reach the Primate House, I'm so tired in this mammal body
I sit with my head against the glass above the gorilla enclosure

and almost miss the newborn gorilla below, tucked in with mama
and nursing from one side then the other, the pair a shared mass

of fur and matching skin. I've weaned my second son,
and he will be the last. My breasts still ache with a sympathetic thud

as mama leans back against the zoo grass and baby latches
as on so many days at school when class ran over and students lingered,

debating grades or making excuses, while my pump was locked inside my office
and my breasts hardened with useless milk. My boys pull my hands,

they're bored of monkeys, they want to ride the train
that goes only in circles and eat a soft pretzel in the sunshine

while the geese beg and make the baby cry. My husband flaps his arms
like an enormous fowl and the kids all laugh: a man pretending

to be a bird. A woman becomes a mother. There will be
no more babies, not for us. I watch the women at the carousel,

their bellies full of daughters, watch the women
clipping their girls' hair back with barrettes. Practice saying *never,*

no more, never, no new babies, no daughters.

Mother Tongue

Corpus luteum doesn't mean
body of light. Early mornings I sat in a second-floor classroom
   learning to scan the meter of a language gone untongued

hundreds of years. I loved the math of it,
     the even rhythms English can't match, caesura and synecdoche
   and all the Roman gods lining up in turn to move the plot. In choir we sang
      dona nobis pacem, pacem, our voices rising and descending
   as we balanced on the risers tapped into place on stage.

   The Romans gave the world
  the *Pax Romana* and filled the known world
with their soldiers. For years I marked time
      across the liturgical calendar, the long march from repentance
   to expectant joy. I was taught to translate *advent* as arrival

but there are other meanings: invasion, and the glorious entry
   of an emperor into a captured city. The *corpus luteum*
     is the shell from which the egg escapes. If unfertilized
   it fades in days, until, one month later a new and newly naked egg
again descends. My sons will never know

   the smell of incense, the solemn steps of altar boys
swinging the censer up and down the aisles. *Lux* is light,
   the clear strong bell of noon sun through stained glass
     behind Christ's body suspended at the altar. My sons

   will never know the quick brightness when the priest says
      go in peace, the shock of sidewalk light
beyond the heavy double doors, the light-bodied moment
   I was taught to name as *grace.*

The News From Happy Valley

When the deleted video resurfaces, the boys are standing around a body.
It's grainy and full of booze, even through the sliced and spliced

and shattered pixels. I've been in those basements—
rickety wooden stairs and a cooler full of jungle juice,

boys in a drunken throng. They're in the central Pennsylvania county
of my birth. When I was born cows roamed the hillside below the hospital window

and those boys were barely a twinkle in their mamas' eyes. Now one of them
has died while the others stood above the body

and did not help. Instead when he is hurt they throw shoes, throw beer,
and one boy slaps him three times, hard. When he still won't wake

they leave him on the couch and his spleen bleeds out
into his belly. The video won't stay deleted. The harm

loops back. When my son pushes
his younger brother to the ground then says

sorry sorry sorry. When he takes his brother's finger
and places it deliberately between his teeth. But also

when we leave daycare he insists some days on hugging
each friend in turn, and the boys turn into a pile,

yelling "Huggy! Huggy!" and laughing
and kissing each other on the cheek:

such tenderness. How to make it stay.

The New Domesticity

All the babies we will ever have
are with us in this Tuesday morning kitchen,

eating freezer waffles and sipping milk
through straws. There's wonder here,

and also there are lunches to be packed, baby
carrots sliced and stacked inside nametagged Tupperware,

socks and shoes to be gathered. Is this
the end of sex? All this domestic bliss.

I slice the toaster waffles into bites and strips
while my husband cores the apples

they'll eat at afternoon snack. The old house
of this marriage has original hardwoods

and penny tile in the powder room, a wide front porch,
and cucumbers turning to goo

in the bottom of the produce drawer.
My husband wants me to put the kids to bed

then put on the lingerie, and isn't
that what we all want, to have a switch to flip

from Mother to Woman, or whatever we might call
a woman who still, after nursing and giving birth

and nursing again still wants to be
a vast and fuckable continent?

I don't know if domestic has to be
the opposite of desire. We velcro shoes

and buckle car seats. At night
we check the babies sleeping sweetly in their beds

and then sometimes behind the bedroom's shut door
you kiss me hard, like inside this mother's body

there's a woman in here still.

The Moon Lets Go

Years and years from now the earth will gain
another hour in its day, but I'll be dead then,

and everyone I love will be gone, too. At daycare dropoff,
my boys wave to me but kiss—*mwah! mwah!*—each other

through the pre-K room's goodbye window,
launching each smooch with a sticky hand and smacking it

against the glass. The moon is small and bound to us by gravity
that's slowly loosening its grip. I'd wanted them to love each other like this.

Goldilocks Zone

The universe is full of amazing things, and if
the *National Geographic Little Kids' First Big Book of Space*
can be believed, many of them are shaped just like

root vegetables: the dwarf planets out past Pluto, the lumpy moons
that orbit Mars, and so, paging through space at bedtime,
when we arrive at the asteroids, my son

points and yells, "Potato!" That we're here at all—
the right distance from a right-sized star, our planet
awash in water and lidded with an atmosphere

that keeps our oxygen here—is an accident
of the most fantastic luck. The world we see
is made of ordinary matter but bound

by darkness we can't measure. In the earliest minutes
it could have been otherwise. The quarks and leptons
and positrons and electrons could, before anything else

began, have simply blinked each other out,
creating instead a universe of light
from horizon to horizon, no sunrise and no stars

and no place to sit and watch the constellations
spin and blink above us. No us. I could so easily
have missed this. Every Tuesday for a whole semester

I stood on the stone patio between classes and bummed cigarettes
from a handsome serious man just so, as he passed the pack of Marlboros,
I could touch his hand. Now you are one half

of the best of each of us. There's no good way
to think about the beginning before the beginning, the universe that burst
somehow from the head of a pin. Where were you

before you were born, before you swam inside my body,
before you cracked me open, before I knew I'd been waiting for you
all those years? The universe today

is bigger and cooler than yesterday. Today when you sit on my lap
your feet all but touch the floor. I am sorry I could not
love you better when you were small. Tonight, before sleep,

you touch your nose to my nose. I think how many worlds
we could have been born into instead. And here we are in this one.

Dark Matter

My daughter broke my back in labor
  is the kind of thing women say to you
over pink-frosted birthday cake, above the din of four year olds
  after you have children

   and so, while we eat the pizza crusts off our children's plates
the mothers commiserate about the shared failings
of our postpartum bodies—how, in the weeks after birth,
hair fell out in clumps that clogged the shower,
  how even the same pounds

sit differently around labor-shifted hips. When I was young,
  I had no idea how many things there were
to be bad at: prompt return of paperwork,
  patience with automated phone menus,

   regular bang trims and dental exams. And also
the things that actually matter: breastfeeding, for example,
  my nipples three days after giving birth so cracked and bleeding
that even the lactation specialist and her nurse

took a startled step back when I unhooked my bra. It is so hard
  to live inside a body. But as I watch the woman whose daughter broke her back
wipe frosting from the cheeks of the son she gave birth to afterward
  my heart is caught by our collective unbearable luck. And then,

   as if the simple act of wishing another year of happiness,
of eating cake and leaping through the bounce house
  is too much joy to bear,
the children close their eyes and sing.

acknowledgments

Grateful acknowledgment to the editors of the following journals, where poems from this collection first appeared:

Blackbird: "Ordinary Pleasure" and "The Braided Stream"; *Broadsided Press:* "Dark Matter"; *Cherry Tree:* "In the Hôtel-Dieu," "My Sentimental Baby," and "The Thing (1982)"; *Colorado Review:* "Ghosts in the Nursery," "The Fifth Great Ape," and "On the First Night of the Afterlife"; *Diode:* "First Light" and "The Sun King Invents Stirruped Birth"; *Eco Theo:* "Feast Day" and "Naming the World"; *EX/POST:* "The News from Happy Valley"; *Foundry:* "Your Best Post-Baby Body"; *The Gettysburg Review:* "Anatomical Venus" and "Goldilocks Zone"; *The Kenyon Review:* "After Cocktail Hour; *The Missouri Review:* "Spooky Action at a Distance," "Twilight," "The Russian Method," "New Year New You," "The Universe has a Temperature"; *NELLE:* "The Middle Sin" and "And Not by Sight"; *Ninth Letter:* "The End of Limbo"; *Poetry is Currency:* "The Good Enough Mother" and "Goodnight Mother, Goodnight Moon"; *Smartish Pace:* "The Nature of Love"; *SWIMM Every Day:* "A Universe Composed of Solely Light"; *Tinderbox Poetry Journal:* "Fable" and "Postpartum"; *Tupelo Quarterly:* "Golden Hour"; *West Review:* "The New Domesticity."

"The Moon Lets Go" was featured in the New York Public Library's Poem in Your Pocket Day celebration for National Poetry Month in April 2019.

"Naming the World" was republished in *ALL Review*'s How to Live series on April 10, 2020

"In the Hôtel-Dieu" was republished on *Poetry Daily* on May 12, 2020.

"Ordinary Pleasure" and "Postpartum" were selected for inclusion in the anthology *Stay Thirsty Poets,* vol. II.

"The Moon Lets Go" and "Your Best Post-Baby Body" were selected for inclusion in the anthology *Welcome to the Resistance: Poetry as Protest,* published by Stockton University Press.

⌒

The poems in this book grew alongside my own children, and so my thanks extend across the people and groups and institutions that have made my writing and mothering possible.

My endless gratitude to the caregivers who loved and taught my children while I worked, including Cathy Empereur, Chery Sachetti and the staff at Ventnor Montessori School, the staff at Haddon Learning Center, the teachers and administrators at Thomas Sharp Elementary School and James A. Garfield Elementary, and the staff at Just Kids aftercare. This past year of remote learning during the pandemic has given me a practical introduction to the challenges of early literacy instruction, and I'm so grateful to the teachers who've taught my sons to love reading and writing.

Dr. Stephanie Skladzien and the Aspen Care Team nurses cared for our family through two pregnancies and births and countless well-baby visits. Our doula, Johanna Hatch, supported us through a long first birth and was the first person through the door after a very quick second birth.

My Madison writing group—Rebecca Dunham, Jesse Lee Kercheval, Cynthia Marie Hoffman, Rita Mae Reese, and Angela Voras-Hills—read the very first of these poems and saw me through the earliest days of motherhood and making my way back into a writing life. Thanks especially to Rebecca and Cynthia for their generous feedback on this manuscript.

The faculty of the PhD program in Composition and Rhetoric at the University of Wisconsin–Madison, where I was a student through my earliest years of motherhood, helped make the multiple identities of scholar/poet/mother/teacher possible. I am particularly grateful for Christa Olson's mentorship.

With thanks to Emily Pérez, for her friendship and editorial partnership.

Ongoing gratitude to Alex Lemon, whose support for my work has meant the world to me.

Thanks and admiration to Nicole Cooley, whose writing and mentorship and kindness has lit the path for me and so many other poets writing through motherhood.

With thanks to the institutions who supported this work: Stockton University's Research and Professional Development Committee and the Provost's Faculty Opportunity Fund, the New Jersey Council on the Arts, the Sustainable Arts Foundation, and the Sewanee Writers' Conference. At Sewanee I had the very good fortune to work with Mark Jarman, whose feedback on an early version of this manuscript was both incisive and kind. Tony and Caroline Grant have done so much to support the creative lives of artists with children, and a grant from the Sustainable Arts Foundation helped me to have faith in the earliest stages of this book.

I'm thankful for my colleagues in the First Year Studies and Writing programs at Stockton University, who've created a truly family friendly program in a field that is often unfriendly to women with children. I'm particularly grateful for Emari DiGiorgio and Emily Van Duyne's friendship and mentorship.

My writing life in New Jersey has been greatly enriched by Murphy Writing, particularly by the Winter Poetry and Prose Getaway, where several of these poems first took shape.

Thanks and appreciation to the team at LSU Press, including James Long. I'm so grateful my work has found a home at LSU Press alongside so many other books I've long admired.

Gratitude and love to the women who've mothered me, and who taught me how to mother, especially my mother, Marilyn Seigh, and my stepmother, Ellen Reddy. For many Tuesdays, Ana Lincoln and Lauren Reynolds took turns holding a fussy baby so I could eat a biscuit or a homemade pop tart. I don't know how to say how much appreciate the generosity of their friendship during that time. Heather Bowlan, voice of encouragement and lava-dance partner, I'm so happy we're on this new journey together, just one river apart.

Endless love to my sons, Penn and Finn. I am so lucky to be your mama. And love to Smith, without whom none of this is possible.

Perinatal mood and anxiety disorders affect many new mothers and often go undiagnosed and untreated. Women struggling with postpartum anxiety and OCD often have particular difficulty accessing effective treatment and support. Postpartum Support International—800-944-4773 or www.postpartum.net—is a good place to start getting help.

notes

Several of the poems in this book were shaped by my research in the history of birth; Randi Hutter Epstein's *Get Me Out* and Tina Cassidy's *Birth* were particularly informative. "Twilight" refers to an incident described in a 1914 *McClure's Magazine* article in which a mother who delivered via twilight sleep refused to recognize the newborn as her own; I learned about this story via Cassidy's book. "The Russian Method" mentions Ivan Pavlov, famous for his experiments with dogs; using that principle, Pavlov then developed a method of pain relief for laboring women. Ferdinand Lamaze, originator of the Lamaze Method, observed Pavlov's "Russian Method" during a visit to the USSR in 1951 and then brought it to the US. *Painless Childbirth* is the title of Lamaze's book. One thread through the history of birth is men blaming women for the pain they experience. Obstetrician Grantly Dick-Read, whose 1942 book *Childbirth Without Fear* helped popularize "natural" childbirth in the US, argued that birth was easy for "normal women"; it was only "psychoneurotic" women who suffered during labor.

The phrase "first light" refers to the first image taken with a new telescope. At the time I wrote this poem, I was reading about the Giant Magellan Telescope being built in Chile; first light for the GMT is currently projected for 2029.

The italicized text in "New Year New You" comes from Gilles Deleuze and Félix Guattari's *A Thousand Plateaus: Capitalism and Schizophrenia*, translated by Brian Massumi.

The poems on space owe a debt to an esoteric bunch of sources, including George Musser's *Spooky Action at a Distance*, Karen Barad's *Meeting the Universe Halfway*, J. Richard Gott and Neil deGrasse Tyson's *Welcome to the Universe*, National Geographic's *Little Kids First Big Book of Space*, *The Cat in the Hat Knows a Lot about Space*, and my sons' wonder at the natural world.

"Anatomical Venus" was informed by Zoe Williams's 2016 *Guardian* article "Cadavers in Pearls: Meet the Anatomical Venus," which observes that "In so many of these figures, almost all of them pregnant, the woman's face is so ideal-ised and the foetus so carefully rendered that she looks like the doll, and the baby like the human."

"The Nature of Love" invokes Harry Harlow's infamous studies using rhesus macaque infants to understand maternal attachment and the impact of maternal deprivation. The poem takes its title from Harlow's "Address of the President at the Annual Convention of the American Psychological Association" in Wash-ington, DC, in August 1958. At this talk, which included still images of the infant monkeys with their cloth mothers, graphs showing contact time across different experimental conditions, and a twenty-minute film demonstrating the experi-ments, Harlow described their cloth mother as "a mother with infinite patience, a mother available twenty-four hours a day, a mother that never scolded her infant and never struck or bit her baby in anger." He asserted that they had engineered a "very superior monkey mother" before joking that "this position is not held uni-versally by the monkey fathers." A portion of Harlow's research was conducted in the basement of the building at the University of Wisconsin in Madison where, years later, I attended graduate school. Deborah Blum's *Love at Goon Park* was an invaluable source in understanding Harlow's work.

"The Braided Stream" was shaped by two news stories from 2015 and 2016: the discovery of the bodies of former EastEnders actress Sian Blake and her sons, ultimately determined to have been murdered and buried by the boys' father; and the discovery of *Homo naledi*, a human ancestor believed to have buried its dead. The fossil evidence of *Homo naledi* was uncovered in an underground cave system in South Africa called Rising Star. I read about *Homo naledi* in a *National Geographic* article, "This Face Changes the Human Story. But How?" by Jamie Shreeve, and in the Berger et al. paper, "*Homo naledi*, A New Species of the Genus *Homo* from the Dinaledi Chamber, South Africa," announcing the discovery in the journal *eLife*. The poem takes its title from paleoanthropologist Lee Berger's suggestion that, rather than thinking of evolution as a tree beginning with a single root and branching out, we instead use of the metaphor of the "braided stream," which splits and then merges again downstream.

"Ghosts in the Nursery" takes its title from the 1975 article by psychoanalysts Selma Fraiberg, Edna Adelson, and Vivian Shapiro, which begins "In every nurs-ery there are ghosts. They are the visitors from the unremembered past of the parents, the uninvited guests at the christening."

"Fable" responds to the 2014 kidnapping of 276 girls from their school in Chibok, Nigeria, by Boko Haram.

"The Good Enough Mother" engages Donald Winnicott's theory of the "good enough parent" or "ordinary good mother," a theory that is not as flexible or forgiving as it's often portrayed. In the 1961 paper "The Theory of the Parent-Infant Relationship," for example, Winnicott asserted that "mothers who have it in them to provide good enough care can be enabled to do better by being cared for themselves in a way that acknowledges the essential nature of their task." However, "mothers who do not have it in them to provide good enough care cannot be made good enough by mere instruction."

"The End of Limbo" references the Catholic Church's International Theological Commission's 2007 publication of "The Hope of Salvation for Infants Who Die Without Being Baptised," which eliminated the concept of purgatory and determined that unbaptized babies could go to heaven. The poem was inspired in part by Michelle Tsai's *Slate* article by the same name.

"The Fifth Great Ape" takes its title from a quotation from Richard Leakey, which I discovered as an epigraph in Sarah Blaffer Hrdy's *Mothers and Others*. The full quotation reads "had humanity not been the interested party, we would have been the fifth great ape."

"The News from Happy Valley" responds to Timothy Piazza's 2017 hazing death at a Penn State fraternity.

CPSIA information can be obtained
at www.ICGtesting.com
Printed in the USA
LVHW112353110522
718572LV00004B/335